THE HEALING YOUR
GRIEVING HEART
JOURNAL
FOR TEENS

Also by Alan Wolfelt:

A Teen's View of Grief:
An Educational Videotape for Bereavement Caregivers

Healing a Child's Grieving Heart:
100 Practical Ideas for Families, Friends and Caregivers

Healing a Parent's Grieving Heart:
100 Practical Ideas After Your Child Dies

Healing a Teen's Grieving Heart:
100 Practical Ideas for Families, Friends and Caregivers

Healing the Bereaved Child:
Grief Gardening, Growth Through Grief and Other
Touchstones for Caregivers

Healing Your Grieving Heart for Kids:
100 Practical Ideas

Healing Your Grieving Heart for Teens:
100 Practical Ideas

How I Feel:
A Coloring Book for Grieving Children

Companion Press is dedicated to the education and support of both the bereaved and bereavement caregivers.

We believe that those who companion the bereaved by walking with them as they journey in grief have a wondrous opportunity: to help others embrace and grow through grief—and to lead fuller, more deeply-lived lives themselves because of this important work.

Companion
P R E S S

THE HEALING YOUR GRIEVING HEART

JOURNAL

FOR TEENS

ALAN D. WOLFELT, PH.D.
MEGAN E. WOLFELT

FOREWORD BY BRIAN GRIESE

Companion
P R E S S

Fort Collins, Colorado
An imprint of the Center for Loss and Life Transition

Companion Press is an imprint of the Center for Loss and Life Transition, 3735 Broken Bow Road, Fort Collins, Colorado 80526

Companion Press books may be purchased in bulk for sales promotions, premiums or fundraisers. Please contact the publisher at the above address for more information.

Printed in the United States of America
11 10 09 08 07 06 05 04 03 02   5 4 3 2 1

ISBN: 1-879651-33-5

Contents

FOREWORD

Someone important in your life has died and your life is different without him or her. I know this from my own personal experience. You see, when I was 12, my mother died from breast cancer. Like yours, my world was changed forever.

How do you survive the powerful thoughts and feelings of loss and grief? How can you remember your past while still hoping for the future? How can you take your grief from inside your heart to outside your heart? How can you carry on and find meaning and purpose in your life?

The Healing Your Grieving Heart Journal for Teens is a guided journal that will help you work through your loss. It will provide you with a "safe place" to learn about your grief and to express your many thoughts and feelings. The pages that follow give you space to write out your memories and provide activities to help you make sense of your grief and find ways to rebuild your life.

As I read this journal, it made me think about how helpful it would have been for me to have something like this during my teen years. I wish I had "thought starters" back then. If I had, I know it would have helped me as I mourned my mom's death and continued to remember her life.

I have no doubt that this journal will help you express important thoughts and feelings and capture memories that you can hold in your heart forever. As Alan and Megan have written, "This journal is an invitation to pour out your heart, to cry, to allow yourself to hurt, and more important, to believe in yourself." I know this journal can and will help you believe in yourself.

This journal will help you think and feel deeply about your special person who has died, about yourself and about your life. If you're already a journal keeper, you know what I'm talking about. If you've never kept a journal, I really suggest you give this one a try!

Alan and Megan Wolfelt are uniquely qualified to bring you this journal. Like me and you, when they were children and teens they both had people they cared about die. They both know that dealing with death is very hard work. They both know that it is important to have "safe places" to explore your experiences with grief. They both know it's important to find ways to go on living.

As you work through this journal, remember—you are not alone. Your grief may feel scary or sad or mad right now, but this journal can make things less scary or sad or mad. Your unique story will unfold in the following pages and you will honor and embrace your grief. You will realize you have been changed by it, but slowly, over time, arrive at a place where life is more full, more fun and more happy than you ever thought possible.

Whatever you do, don't give up. You'll find yourself: the new you. And I think you will like what you find!

Take care,

Brian Griese
Quarterback, Denver Broncos

A NOTE FROM MEGAN

Sooner of later death will be part of everyone's life. Unfortunately for me, death became a part of my life when I was in first grade. One of my best friends, Jeremy Becker, and I liked to chase each other around the playground at recess. He was a very nice boy. Then one afternoon, after he had helped me carry a project to my car, he was hit by a car while walking home from school. That night my mom told me that he had been killed. I still remember how sad I was.

Later, when I was 11 , my grandpa died. He lived far away and I didn't get to see him that often, but I was still very sad when he died. You can still love somebody even if they live far away from you. Grandpa came to our house for Christmas a lot and he was great to spend the holidays with. Now I wish I could have had a chance to get to know him better as I was growing up.

Luckily for me, I have my mom and my dad to talk to about my feelings. My dad is a grief counselor and he travels the country speaking about healing in grief. He taught me that I shouldn't be afraid to talk about death. He also taught me that writing about my thoughts and feelings is a good way to express them and learn from them. That's why we put together this journal—to help you get your grief outside of yourself.

I hope you'll use this book to say whatever you're thinking and feeling. Remember that your feelings are OK, no matter what they are. And if you talk about your feelings with people you love and write about them and express them in ways that feel right to you, you'll be OK, too.

Megan E. Wolfelt

Megan Wolfelt
Age 14

So you musn't be frightened . . . if a sadness rises in front of you larger than anything you have ever seen. . . You must realize that something is happening to you, that life has not forgotten you, that it holds you in its hand and will not let you fall.

Rainer Maria Rilke
Letters to a Young Poet

INTRODUCTION

We have written this journal just for you and teens like you. It is a special place for you to share your thoughts and feelings. Within the pages that follow, you can remember, celebrate and commemorate the life of the person to whom this journal is dedicated.

Our hope is that this guided journal can be a "safe place" for you to explore your experiences with grief. As you tell your story, your words will guide you on your personal, unique journey through the healing experience of grief. As your words bring life to these pages, you will be giving testimony to the love you will always have for the person who has died.

Because you are a teen and because you're unique, you're very special. This is an exciting stage of your life. The changes you're going through physically, emotionally, intellectually and spiritually can be exciting but also overwhelming. You're not a kid anymore. You're not an adult, yet, either. Others may expect you to act, think and feel like an adult, but much of your childhood, thankfully, is still inside you.

So when someone you love dies, it can be more difficult for you now that at any other age. When someone close to us dies, we begin a journey, a journey not of our choosing and with no exact course. It's hard to understand and cope with all the feelings that accompany grief along with the changes your body and mind are going through. In some ways these feelings are similar; both can cause your moods to swing unexpectedly. Both can make you feel out of control of your life.

We're so sorry you have lost someone who meant a lot to you— perhaps even the world. While we cannot think and feel exactly what you are, we do want you to know we have both been there. We both experienced the deaths of friends and family early in our lives. Like we did, you may feel very sad or hurt right now. Perhaps you're angry. Or depressed. Maybe you feel lost or deserted. Maybe for the first time you really realize that we all die. All these feelings are part of grieving and are OK to feel.

Let us explain the very important difference between grief and mourning. Grief is what you think and feel on the inside when someone you love dies. Mourning is the expression of these thoughts and feelings—letting them out somehow. You mourn when you talk to other people about your grief, when you cry, when you look at photos of the person who died, when you visit the cemetery or when you write about your feelings in a journal like this. You may be grieving like crazy inside but unless you let out those powerful thoughts and feelings—unless you mourn—you won't truly heal.

Journaling has proven to be an excellent way for many teens to do the work of mourning. Journaling is private and independent, yet it's still expressing your grief outside of yourself. I've been a grief counselor for a long time (almost 20 years!), and I've found that journaling helps grieving people:

• clarify what you're thinking and feeling.
• have a safe place of solace, a best friend, a place where you can fully express yourself no matter how sad, scared, confused or lonely you feel.
• strengthen your self-awareness of how your grief journey changes over time. It can be amazing to go back months and years later and read what you have written and realize how much you have changed. When you pore through these pages even years later, you will remember what your grief journey was like for you and you will cherish what you have written.
• soften the intensity of your thoughts and feelings and help you better understand this journey called grief and mourning.
• clear out your naturally overwhelmed mind and full heart.
• look at the pain you are experiencing and transform it into something survivable.
• create an opportunity to acknowledge the balance in your life between the sad and the happy.
• map out your growth as you travel into and through the grief journey.

In fact, studies have shown that teens who write on a regular basis about their lives and related thoughts and feelings are healthier people physically, emotionally, socially and spiritually. Simply writing out

8

thoughts and feelings at least four times a week can decrease stress on your immune system and workload on your body.

Write out below three or four reasons you can think of for working on this journal:

1._____
2._____
3._____
4._____

Journaling Suggestions

First, please remember that there is no "correct" or "right" way to use this journal! Yes, we have purposely provided thought starters (we extend invitations to you, but don't make demands of you) to help you have what is called a "guided journal." But, this is only to help you along your path. Give yourself permission to write whatever your head and heart are telling you. Use your imagination and individual creativity. Use colored pens if you want; slip treasured photos or letters between the pages. Cut out and attach an article or image that comforts you. There are many ways to communicate with yourself and the spirit of the person who has died. Tap into all the ways that work for you. Do expect ups and down. Many teens report an increase in sad feelings when they begin writing about the death of someone loved. That's OK. Keep writing, even through the sadness. It can and will help you begin to heal!

What is a journal?

Some teens have taught us that it helps to define what a journal is. This journal is your account of the life and death of someone special to you and how you think and feel about it. It is usually hand-written, but you can also type on a computer or record your thoughts and feelings onto a cassette or CD. The "journaler"—that's you—can decide which method is best. Keeping a journal is not the same as keeping a diary. A diary records events as they happen, usually on a daily basis. A journal is a record of thoughts, feelings and memories over a longer period of time. This way, over the weeks, months and years you will see patterns, notice changes and progress, and monitor your growth.

Setting

Pick a private place to write and store your journal. Naturally, journaling is usually easier to do in a quiet place. You should be free from interruptions and distractions. Most teens have taught us that they like to journal in their bedroom, but you should pick the place that works for you.

Time

You probably have a busy schedule with school, friends and activities. Your journal isn't something you have to write in every day. Yet, the more often you use this journal, particularly in the beginning, the more benefit you will get from it. Maybe you have a time of day that is best for you—early in the morning or right after school or just before bed. Be your own judge about how much time you spend writing in your journal on a particular day. One day you may write a lot; another time you may simply sit and think. That's the beauty of a journal; you can write whenever you feel like it. There's no pressure, no timetable and no absolute deadline.

Honesty

In an effort to understand yourself and your grief journey, you must be honest with yourself. This journal is a place to truly be yourself—think your real thoughts and share them, feel your true feelings and express them.

Privacy

This is your journal and it is private and confidential. You have every right to your privacy. Remember—you don't have to share your journal or show it to anyone you don't want to. So, keep your journal in a safe, private place. Tell your family and friends that your journal is personal and private.

Selective Sharing

It's important to let others help you with your grief. Now, we understand that you may not want help. You are a teenager and one of your main tasks in life is to become more independent and handle things on your own. Nature designed it that way so you'll learn how to fend for and make a life for yourself. But grief is an exception; you

can't cope with it alone (nobody can, not even adults) and you
shouldn't try to. As hard as it is, you need to let others be there
for you

This said, you may want to share a particular journal entry with
someone you trust—a best friend, a parent, a teacher or a counselor.
When we say someone you trust, we mean someone who accepts you
where you are right now in your grief journey. This means they don't
judge you or think their job is to "get you over grief" quickly.

The purpose of this kind of guided journal is, in part, to help you
learn to understand your grief and become friends with it. If you are
around people who judge or criticize you, it's hard to mourn openly
and honestly. Critical people aren't likely to understand you or your
journal so we suggest you do not share your journal with them. But
selectively sharing your journal with people you love and trust can
help them understand what you're thinking and feeling. It can also
help them understand how they can (and can't) support you in your
journey through grief.

Getting Started

When you are ready to start exploring this journal, find the right place
that feels comfortable (we hope you have already done this as you
read this Introduction). Quiet yourself and try to just relax. You may
want to have a few moments of silence before you begin so that you
can focus your attention on what you are going to do in the journal.
When you feel relaxed, slowly close your eyes and reopen them. Now
you are ready to begin.

Oh, before you begin, remember this: Don't criticize what you find
comes to the paper. Ignore your penmanship and don't worry about
grammar or spelling (you have to do that enough in school!). This
journal is just for you!

Godspeed to You

Please take care of yourself and be patient as you explore this journal.
With time and the support of others, you will come to feel hope and a
renewed excitement for life and living. This journal is an invitation to

pour out your heart, to cry, to allow yourself to hurt, and most important, to believe in yourself. A journal is a confessor. It simply listens as you write. And it may be hard to believe this now, but you'll also emerge wiser, more sensitive and more complete than you were before. Believe in your ability to grow and heal. Believe in God's plan for you on this earth. Good luck and Godspeed.

So what are you waiting for? Pick up your pen and get started! Months and even years from now, you'll be glad you did.

All the best,

Alan D. Wolfelt   Megan E. Wolfelt

My name:_____

Name of the person who died:_____

I started this journal on this day_____

in the year_____ in the city of_____ when I

was _____ years old.

I finished this journal on this day _____

in the year_____ when I was _____ years old.

This journal is special to me because...

_____

_____

_____

_____

_____

_____

_____

_____

_____

_____

_____

_____

_____

_____

_____

_____

_____

Here's a photograph of my special person who has died:

This picture is special to me because...
_____
_____
_____
_____

GETTING STARTED:
WHY YOUR GRIEF IS WHAT IT IS

Surrounded by my memories . . . I took my pen and began to write.
Kuki Gullman

This guided journal is a safe place for you to express your many thoughts, feelings and memories. In part, it is an exploration of how someone's death has changed your life. Our hope is that this journal will help you in your healing and honor your relationship with someone who has been a special part of your world.

Your unique grief journey will be shaped by many things. No two deaths are ever mourned in exactly the same way. Don't think you should grieve in a certain way. Your grief is what it is. It's your right to express it.

Despite what you may hear, you will do the "work of mourning" in your own way. Be careful not to compare your experience with that of other teens. Consider taking a "one-day-at-a-time" approach. Doing so will allow you to mourn at your own pace.

This section of your journal will allow you to explore some of the unique reasons your grief is what it is. Following each "why," we have created some questions for you to answer. As you journal out your responses, we believe you will discover more about the uniqueness of your grief.

You can do it—just write down some of your thoughts and feelings following the questions in the spaces provided.

Why #1:
Your Relationship with the Person Who Died

As you know, your relationship with the person who died was different than that person's relationship with anyone else. For example, you may have been "best friends" or "Daddy's little girl." Or perhaps you loved the person but had lots of hard times with him or her. Maybe you were separated by physical distance, which kept you from being as close as you would have liked. Whatever the situation, you are the best person to describe your relationship with the person who died.

Who has died?

_____

In general, how would you describe your relationship to this person?

_____

_____

_____

_____

_____

_____

How attached were you to this person?

_____

_____

_____

_____

_____

Describe how you showed this attachment to each other:

_____

_____

_____

_____

_____

_____

_____

_____

_____

_____

_____

Can you remember times when you felt very close to this person? Please describe/explain.

_____

_____

_____

_____

_____

_____

_____

_____

_____

_____

_____

Were there times when it was hard to get along with this person? If so, give some examples of those times. If not, write about why you think you got along so well.

_____

_____

_____

_____

_____

_____

_____

_____

_____

_____

_____

_____

What did this person look like?

Approximate height_____ Approximate weight_____

Hair color_____   Eye color_____

Other distinguishing characteristics:

_____

_____

_____

_____

_____

_____

_____

Place another favorite photo of the person who died right here:

Write about two special memories you will always have of
your relationship with the person who died:

_____

_____

_____

_____

_____

_____

_____

_____

_____

_____

_____

_____

_____

_____

_____

_____

_____

_____

_____

_____

_____

_____

_____

_____

Why #2:
The Circumstances of the Death

The unique circumstances of the death of someone in your life can have a real impact on your grief journey. For example, was the death anticipated or was it sudden and unexpected? How old was the person who died? Was the death painful or painless? Do you feel like you should have been able to do something to prevent the death? Even when you know someone is dying, you can never really be prepared. We're never ready for the death of someone we love. If the person was sick for a long time and you knew that he or she was going to die, the death may still feel unreal and shocking to you.

Describe the circumstances of the death:

_____

_____

_____

_____

How did you learn about the death?

_____

_____

_____

_____

Was the death something you expected to happen or was it sudden and unexpected? How does this affect your grief?

_____

_____

_____

_____

How old was the person who died?_____
How does the age of the person affect your grief?

_____

_____

What questions, if any, do you still have about how or why
the person died?

_____

_____

_____

_____

_____

_____

Who could answer these questions for you? (If you have
questions, ask! It's not good to let them fester inside you.)

_____

_____

What other thoughts and feelings come to mind when you
think about how this person died?

_____

_____

_____

_____

_____

_____

Why #3:
The People In Your Life

As you have already learned, you need help from others if you are to heal your grief. Without really good support from your family, friends, teachers, coaches, etc., it's hard to do your mourning. Your healing needs and deserves lots of gentle, caring encouragement and love.

Friends are especially important during your teenage years. And when you're grieving, your friends can be extra especially important. We realize that you may not feel like being around people when you're sad or depressed over losing someone. But now, more than ever, friends can come to your aid. Even if you have nothing to say, or your friends don't know what to say to you, their mere presence can help you feel loved and supported.

What about your family? You may or may not feel like confiding in them right now. That's normal for teenagers! But still, we hope your family loves you and wants what's best for you. During the course of your life, your friends may come and go but your family is forever. Let your family be there for you. Let them in, even if it's hard for you. Try to be open and honest with your family about your grief.

Do you have people in your life whom you can turn to for help and support? Who?

_____

_____

_____

_____

_____

_____

_____

What qualities do these people have that make them seem approachable and "safe"?

_____

_____

_____

_____

_____

Are there some people in your life you wish you could turn to for support but you don't feel you can? If so, who are these people and why can't you turn to them?

_____

_____

_____

_____

_____

Do you live far away from some people in your life who could help you if they were nearby?
If so, who?_____
Perhaps you could arrange to talk to this person by phone or by e-mail or maybe you could plan a special visit. What ideas do you have for reaching out to this person?

_____

_____

_____

_____

_____

Are you willing to accept support from friends and family?
Yes_____   No_____   If not, why not?

_____

_____

_____

Sometimes well-meaning friends and family will hurt you unknowingly with their words. They may tell you:

- "I know how you feel." (They don't.)
- "Get on with your life." (You're not ready to.)
- "Keep your chin up." (You have every right to be sad.)
- "You're young; you'll get over this. (Nobody ever "gets over" grief.)
- "Time heals all wounds." (Time helps, but you're feeling bad today.)
- "He/she wouldn't want you to be sad." (Death and sadness go hand in hand.)

Have you had anyone say things like this to you?
Yes_____   No_____   If so, write out an example and describe how it made you feel.

_____

_____

_____

_____

_____

_____

_____

_____

What are some things that people have said or done that
have been helpful to you?

_____

_____

_____

_____

_____

_____

_____

_____

_____

_____

Do you have a school counselor, teacher or coach you can
turn to for support? Yes_____ No_____ If so, describe
this special adult and why you feel they can help you.

_____

_____

_____

_____

_____

_____

_____

_____

_____

_____

_____

Do you have a clergyperson or friends at church or a place of worship you can turn to for support?

Yes_____ No_____ Describe these people and this place.

_____

_____

_____

_____

_____

_____

_____

_____

_____

_____

_____

_____

_____

_____

_____

_____

_____

_____

_____

_____

_____

_____

_____

_____

_____

Grief support groups are a safe place for many teens. Sometimes it's easier to talk to other kids whose lives have been touched by death than it is to talk to adults. Have you participated in a support group? Yes_____ No_____ If so, describe this experience:

_____

_____

_____

_____

_____

_____

_____

_____

_____

_____

_____

_____

_____

_____

If you haven't been to a support group, could you find out if there may be one in your area? Your school might have a support group. If not, your place of worship, a hospice or a funeral home may have one. Name an adult who can help you find out about teen grief support groups and arrange to attend:

_____

Why #4:
Your Unique Personality

No one else is just like you. Your unique personality is a big part of your grief. For example, if you are kind of quiet and shy, you may express your grief quietly. If you are outgoing and talkative, you may be more expressive with your grief.

Other things, like your self-esteem, your beliefs and the ways in which you have responded to other losses in your life, also play a part in how you respond to a death. Let's have you write out your responses to the following questions so you can better understand how your unique personality shapes your grief.

What are some adjectives you would use to
describe yourself?

_____   _____

_____   _____

_____   _____

_____   _____

_____   _____

How do you think your unique personality is influencing
your grief?

_____

_____

_____

_____

_____

_____

_____

How have you responded to other life losses or crises in your life?

_____

_____

_____

_____

Are you responding in a similar way now, or does this loss feel different somehow? Explain.

_____

_____

_____

_____

Do you think your personality has changed as a result of this death? Yes_____ No_____
If so, how? If not, why not?

_____

_____

_____

_____

_____

How is your self-esteem right now? Why?

_____

_____

_____

_____

Why #5:
The Unique Personality of the Person Who Died

Just as your unique personality is part of your grief, so, too, is the personality of the person who died. For example, it may be that the person was someone you found easy to like and admire. Or it may be that the person was hard to get along with; you may have loved the person a lot but you may not have always liked them. Check off the following personality traits that seem to describe the person who died:

___ accepting

___ active

___ adventuresome

___ aggressive

___ annoying

___ anxious

___ argumentative

___ artistic

___ big-hearted

___ calm

___ caring

___ charming

___ clever

___ cold

___ compassionate

___ competitive

___ conceited

___ confident

___ controlling

___ cooperative

___ courageous

___ creative

___ critical

___ demanding

___ dependable

___ detached

___ direct

___ dramatic

___ dynamic

___ emotional

___ energetic

___ enthusiastic

___ fair

___ forgetful

___ friendly

___ funny

___ good-natured

___ graceful

___ honest

___ hyperactive

___ imaginative

___ independent

___ inflexible

___ influential

___ insecure

___ interesting

___ inventive

___ irritable

___ jealous

___ logical

___ loud

___ moody

___ nervous

___ nurturing

___ opinionated

___ outgoing

___ overprotective

___ overwhelming

___ perfectionistic

___ persuasive

___ playful

___ protective

___ punctual

___ quick to anger

___ rebellious

___ resourceful

___ rude

___ romantic

___ scatterbrained

___ self-centered

___ sensitive

___ shy

___ sincere

___ smart

___ spiritual

___ spontaneous

___ stubborn

___ temperamental

___ tireless

___ troubled

___ trustworthy

___ two-faced

___ warm

___ wise

___ witty

___ wonderful

___ worried

Now, in your own words, describe the personality of the person who died.

_____

_____

_____

_____

_____

_____

_____

_____

_____

_____

_____

_____

_____

_____

_____

_____

_____

_____

_____

_____

_____

_____

Place a photo of the person who died here that you think expresses his or her unique personality.

What roles did this person play in your life? (For example, best friend, mentor, caretaker.)

_____

_____

_____

_____

_____

_____

_____

How did this person's unique personality affect the roles he or she played in your life?

_____

_____

_____

_____

_____

_____

_____

Which personality traits of this person's did you enjoy most?

_____

_____

_____

_____

_____

_____

Give an example of a time when these positive traits were expressed by this person.

_____

_____

_____

_____

_____

_____

_____

Which personality traits of this person's did you least enjoy?

_____

_____

_____

_____

_____

_____

_____

Give an example of a time when these negative traits were apparent to you.

_____

_____

_____

_____

_____

_____

Why #6:
Your Cultural Background

Your family's culture is an important part of how you experience and express your grief. When we say culture, we mean the values, rules (spoken and unspoken) and traditions that guide your family. Often these values, rules and traditions have been handed down generation after generation and are shaped by the countries or areas of the world your family originally came from. Your family's culture is also shaped by education and political beliefs (religion, too, but we'll get to that in a minute). Basically, your family's culture is your family's way of being in the world.

What is your cultural background?

_____

_____

_____

_____

_____

_____

_____

_____

How does this background influence your grief
and mourning?

_____

_____

_____

_____

_____

Ask a trusted adult about your family's culture. What did you learn about your family's cultural background?

_____

_____

_____

_____

_____

_____

_____

_____

_____

_____

_____

How might this help or hinder you in your journey through grief?

_____

_____

_____

_____

_____

_____

_____

_____

_____

_____

Why #7:
Your Religious or Spiritual Background

Your faith or belief system can be a big influence on your grief. You may discover that your religious or spiritual life is deepened, renewed or changed because of this death. Or you may well find yourself questioning beliefs you used to take for granted.

The word "faith" means to believe in something for which there is no proof. For some people, faith means believing in and following a set of religious rules. For others, faith is a belief in God or a spirit or a force that is greater than we are.

One important point we want you to remember is even if you have faith, you still have a need and a right to mourn. Your religion may teach you that God is all-knowing and that this death is part of His plan. It may also teach you that the person who died has gone to a better place and so you should be happy for him or her. Even if these things are true, an important person has been torn from your life and you need to mourn the loss.

The following questions may help you understand how your religious and spiritual beliefs affect your grief journey.

Did you grow up with certain religious or spiritual teachings? Please describe them.

_____

_____

_____

_____

_____

_____

_____

Do you believe in God? Yes_____ No_____

What do you believe happens after death?

_____

_____

_____

_____

Has this death impacted your faith? How?

_____

_____

_____

_____

_____

Do you have people around you who understand and support you in your belief system? Yes_____ No_____

If so, who are these people and how can they help you?

_____

_____

_____

_____

Do you think that your faith, religion or spiritual background will play a part in your healing process?

Yes_____ No_____ Please explain.

_____

_____

_____

Why #8:
Other Crises or Stresses in Your Life

The death of someone in your life often brings about other losses. In grief counseling, we call these "secondary losses." Besides the death, you may also experience the loss of long-time friends who abandon you in your grief, the loss of a sense of future, or the loss of your school or neighborhood if you have to move.

You probably also have other stresses in your life right now. Teenagers are typically very busy and have lots of demands on their time. School, sports, jobs and activities can make your life hectic. Love interests and social challenges can stress you out, too.

Allow the following questions to help you better understand how other crises, losses or stresses make your grief what it is.

What other losses have come about in your life either as a result of the death or coincidentally during the same time frame?

_____

_____

_____

_____

_____

How do you see these other losses influencing your grief?

_____

_____

_____

_____

_____

What other stresses or crises are a part of your life right now?

_____

_____

_____

_____

_____

_____

_____

How are they affecting your grief?

_____

_____

_____

_____

_____

_____

_____

_____

_____

Whom can you turn to right now to help you cope with these secondary losses or stresses?

_____

_____

_____

_____

Why #9:
Your Gender

Your gender affects not only your grief, but also how people relate to you at this time. Often boys are expected to "be strong" after a death. As a result, some boys find it hard to allow themselves to express their sadness. Girls sometimes find it hard to express feelings of anger, while boys tend to be more quick to get mad.

After a death in the family, both boys and girls are often forced to grow up too quickly. You may be asked to take on adult responsibilities. You may be told you need to be the "man" or "woman" of the house now.

Do you think that being a boy or a girl affects your grief?
Yes_____ No_____ If so, how?

_____

_____

_____

_____

_____

_____

_____

_____

_____

_____

_____

_____

_____

_____

Has your gender influenced how people support you in your grief? If so, how?

_____

_____

_____

_____

_____

_____

_____

_____

_____

_____

_____

In grief, do you see any advantages or disadvantages to being the gender you are?

_____

_____

_____

_____

_____

_____

_____

_____

_____

_____

_____

_____

Why #10:
The Funeral Experience

We hope you were able to be part of a meaningful funeral or memorial service for the person who died. A good funeral can help you begin to honor your memories, bring you closer to others who can give you support and give you a safe time and place to embrace your religious or spiritual beliefs. If you didn't get to attend the funeral, it's never too late after a death to plan and carry out a ritual that will help you meet your needs. For example, you could have a tree-planting ceremony in memory of the person who died or you could plan a memorial service on the anniversary of the death. You deserve it, and so does the special person in your life who died.

Did you attend a funeral for the person who died?

Yes_____ No_____ If so, describe what this experience was like for you.

_____

_____

_____

_____

_____

_____

If you were not able to be a part of the funeral, how do you feel about that?

_____

_____

_____

_____

_____

Do you feel a need to create an additional ritual that would help you with your grief? Yes_____ No_____

If so, who could you turn to to help you make plans to do this?_____

What ideas do you have for creating a ceremony?

_____
_____
_____
_____
_____
_____
_____
_____
_____

In what ways can you continue to use ceremony to remember other special times, such as the birthday of the person who died or the anniversary of the death?

_____
_____
_____
_____
_____
_____
_____
_____
_____
_____
_____

As we noted in the beginning of this section, your unique grief will be shaped by many things. We have reviewed some of these "whys" with you. Now, in the space below, we encourage you to write about any other things that you believe might be affecting what you are thinking and feeling right now.

_____

_____

_____

_____

_____

_____

_____

_____

_____

_____

_____

_____

_____

_____

_____

_____

_____

_____

_____

_____

_____

_____

EXPLORING YOUR
FEELINGS OF LOSS

"There is no right response to death. You make it up as you go along."
Joan Lonner

The death of someone you love affects your head, heart and spirit. Grief often involves a wide range of feelings, from disbelief and sadness to anger, frustration, confusion, loneliness and more. Experiencing these emotions, and sometimes feeling overwhelmed by them, is a natural part of the grief process.

We like to describe grief like waves coming in from the ocean. At times, the waves are small and barely noticeable. But when you least suspect it, a huge wave may pull your feet right out from under you. No two people ever see these waves exactly the same way, and no one reacts in the same way to each incoming wave.

As strange as your emotions may seem, they are a true expression of where you are right now. Rather than deny or feel victimized by your feelings, we want to help you learn to recognize and learn from them. Naming the feelings and acknowledging them are the first steps to dealing with them.

Also, don't be surprised if you suddenly experience surges of grief, even at the most unexpected times. These griefbursts can be frightening and leave you feeling overwhelmed. They are, however, a natural response to the death of someone loved. You're not weird. You're not the only one. You're not crazy.

A great way to take care of yourself is to become familiar with the thoughts, feelings and behaviors that you may experience in your grief journey. It's actually this process of becoming friendly with your feelings that will help you heal.

Before exploring some of your possible responses to the death of your special person, please take a moment to write out a few words that describe how you are feeling right now. In the space below, complete the following statement:

Right now, I'm feeling. . .

_____

_____

_____

_____

_____

_____

_____

_____

_____

Our goal for this part of the journal is to help you see how normal your grief thoughts, feelings and behaviors are. We will describe of some of what you might be experiencing and then invite you to write out your own personal experiences. Remember—you may not have had all these things we describe, but you may find yourself doing so in the future.

So, here we go...

Shock, numbness, disbelief

Thank goodness for shock, numbness and disbelief. This is nature's way of protecting you from having too many painful feelings all at once. You may feel dazed or stunned during this time. You may feel like it is all a bad dream. Your feelings need time to catch up with what your mind has been told. At some level, you know the person is dead, yet you may not be able or willing to believe it. Your mind may approach and retreat from the reality of the death over and over again as you try to make sense of what has happened. Even after you have moved beyond your initial feelings of shock, numbness and disbelief, don't be surprised if these feelings come up again in future weeks and months. Birthdays, holiday, anniversaries and other special occasions that may only be known to you sometimes trigger these feelings. Again, this is normal. It allows you to be where you are at this moment in time.

My experience with shock, numbness and disbelief is, or has been: _____

_____

_____

_____

_____

_____

_____

_____

_____

_____

Disorganization and confusion

Have you had some trouble with your concentration and memory? If so, we hope you realize you are not alone. Many teens have taught us that disorganization and confusion can be kind of scary. As one 15-year-old said, "I couldn't believe I was so scattered and couldn't remember things."

Sometimes these very normal and natural symptoms can make you think you are "losing it." Just trust that you are not. In grief, thoughts, feelings and behaviors are different from what you normally experience. Disconnected thoughts can race through your mind and strong feelings may be overwhelming.

You may have a hard time concentrating on your schoolwork. You may have a hard time eating or sleeping the way you normally do. You may feel kind of wiped out and drained.

We hope you find it helpful to know that disorganization and confusion after a death come before any kind of reorientation. It's like Helen Keller once said: "The only way to the other side is through." Some people around you may try to have you bypass any kind of disorganization and confusion. Remember—it simply can't be done. While it seems strange, you must descend into your grief before you can transcend out of it. In other words, you must allow yourself to experience the painful thoughts and feelings before you can begin to heal. If you are having, or have had, some of these feelings, try to see them as stepping stones on your path toward healing.

My experience with disorganization and confusion is, or has been: _____

_____

_____

_____

_____

_____

_____

_____

_____

_____

_____

_____

Anxiety, panic, fear

You may have some anxiety, panic and fear as part of your grief journey. You may ask yourself questions like, "Am I going to be OK? Will my family be OK? Will my life have a purpose without this person?" As scary as these questions are, they are normal to ask. Your feelings of safety and security have been threatened, so you naturally feel anxious.

As your head and heart miss the person who was a part of your life, panic may set in. Some teens have even taught us that they feel like they are "going crazy." If you begin to think there is something "wrong" with what you are thinking and feeling, you might get even more frightened. That's why having a place to write out any scary thoughts and feelings is so very important.

Some teens experience fear of what the future holds. You may worry that you won't survive without the person. You may worry about other people dying. Now that you've encountered death, perhaps for the first time, you may begin to fear or worry about your own death. Obviously, anxiety, panic and fear are a normal part of the grief journey for many teens. How about you?

My experience with anxiety, panic and fear is, or has been:

_____

_____

_____

_____

_____

_____

_____

_____

_____

_____

Physical symptoms

Have you noticed how smart your body is? It will let you know when it is distressed. You may be shocked by how much your body responds to the impact of your loss.

Two common physical responses to grief include trouble sleeping and low energy. You may have trouble getting to sleep, or even more likely, you may wake up during the night and have trouble getting back to sleep. Some teens have taught us that they might experience what's called "hypersomnia"—which means you feel like sleeping all the time. If this happens to you, be sure to talk to a trusted adult who can help you get help.

During your grief journey, your body needs more rest than usual. You may find yourself feeling tired more quickly—sometimes even at the start of the day. This is called the "lethargy of grief." It's your body trying to help you slow down and feel your grief.

Some grieving teens have muscle aches and pains, shortness of breath, feelings of emptiness in the stomach, headaches, problems with allergies, agitation or tension. All of these are ways your body may react to the loss of someone loved. Any kind of existing health problem you had before the death may cause you more trouble now. If you have any symptoms that concern or frighten you, the best thing to do is talk to a trusted adult about them and then see your doctor. You're probably just fine, but having your doctor assure you you're fine will give you peace of mind.

Something teens like you really need to watch out for is changes in appetite and weight loss or gain. While it is normal to have your eating patterns be affected by your grief, watch out for any kind of major changes in your eating behaviors. Some teens have or develop eating disorders that are very serious and require medical attention. If this strikes a chord with you, don't hide your problem. Get help now! You're worth it!

Obviously, your body will communicate about the grief stress you are experiencing. You only have one body, so please pay attention to and care for it.

My body is, or has been, responding to the stress of grief by: _____

_____

_____

_____

_____

_____

_____

_____

_____

_____

Explosive emotions

Grieving teens have helped us understand that they sometimes feel a whole range of feelings that can be called "explosive emotions." These include anger, hate, blame, resentment, rage and jealousy. These feelings are your mind's way of trying to survive by protesting the death. Deep down your anger is saying, "I don't like what has happened! I want this person back!"

Your explosive emotions may be kind of scary, yet they are normal and natural. Unfortunately, our society sometimes teaches us that these feelings aren't normal, or that they're wrong. While you must be careful not to "act out" these emotions in destructive ways (i.e. hurting yourself, hurting others, destroying property), we do encourage you to be honest with yourself about what you feel. To deny emotions, even angry ones, is to deny the essence of life.

Remember—these explosive emotions do not have to be logical. They are not good or bad, right or wrong. They simply are. Don't judge your feelings. Instead, experience them and work to understand them in ways that help you heal. For example, it might help you to know that underneath these emotions are often feelings of pain, helplessness, fear and hurt.

While these feelings are normal, know that they should soften as you do the work of mourning. If you are confused by these or any other feelings you are having, we encourage you to reach out to a trusted adult who can understand and support you. Also, put this friendly journal to work right now!

My experience with explosive emotions is, or has been:

_____

_____

_____

_____

_____

_____

_____

_____

_____

_____

Regrets and guilt

As part of your grief journey, you may experience some regrets and guilt. You might have even said or thought things like, "If only I wouldn't have been mean to him." Or, "If only I'd known she wasn't feeling well and I had told her to go the doctor." Or, "If only I'd let him know how much I cared about him." Or, "If only I had told him not to walk home that way on that day."

If you have been thinking some of these "if onlys," don't be so hard on yourself. When someone you care about dies, it's natural to think about actions you could or could not have taken to prevent the death. You simply are unable to go through life in close relationship with other people without saying or doing something you later wish you could change.

Some teens think thoughts can cause actions. This is called "magical thinking." At some point in your relationship with the person who died, you may have thought, "I wish you would go away and leave me alone." Or, if the relationship was very difficult for whatever reason, you may have even hoped it would end forever. If so, you may now feel somehow responsible for the death.

All relationships have periods when negative thoughts occur. Obviously, however, your mind doesn't have the power to inflict death. If you are struggling with guilt, please talk with a caring adult who will be understanding and nonjudgmental.

Don't let feelings of guilt or regret (real or imagined) to go unexpressed. While they are a natural part of your journey, they need to be explored. So get started right now. Write them out in the journal right here, right now.

My experience with regrets and guilt is, or has been:

_____

_____

_____

_____

_____

_____

_____

_____

_____

_____

_____

_____

Loss and sadness

With good reason, feelings of loss and sadness may be a major part of your grief. Someone you love has died and you hurt. Your feelings of loss and sadness are symptoms of your wounds. Just as physical wounds require attention, so do emotional and spiritual wounds. Interestingly enough, the only way to eventually lessen your pain is to move toward it (in small doses), not away from it.

Moving toward your feelings of loss and sadness isn't always easy to do. Sometimes people around you don't like it when you feel these feelings. Some people may even say things like, "Don't be sad" or "You'll have another best friend" or "You still have your mom" or "Well, just think of who you have to be thankful for." Comments like these don't help your healing. If your heart and soul are prevented from feeling the sadness, you can't heal. You must listen and learn from your sadness.

Most grieving teens have taught us that the full sense of loss doesn't come all at once. As you learn to move toward your sadness while getting support from people around you, you will discover meaning and purpose in your life.

Times of loss and sadness for some grieving teens may include bedtime, weekends, holidays, family meals, arriving home to an empty house, and any kind of anniversary occasion. These difficult times usually have a special connection to the person who has died.

Weeks and months may pass before you are fully aware of your feelings of loss and sadness. This slowly growing awareness is good because you may not be able to handle all of your sadness at once. Surround yourself with loving people who understand, not judge you. You have every right to feel loss and sadness.

A SPECIAL WARNING: If you or people around you are concerned that your sadness has grown into what is called depression, go see your family doctor or a trained counselor.

My experience with loss and sadness is, or has been:

_____

_____

_____

_____

_____

_____

_____

_____

_____

_____

Relief and release

Many teens experience feelings of relief and release when someone
dies. These feelings are normal and natural. The death may bring relief
from suffering, particularly when an illness has lasted a long time. Any
feelings of relief and release you may have don't mean you didn't care
about the person who died.

Feelings of relief and release can also relate to how you don't just start
to mourn when someone dies. Often, your grief and mourning start
when someone first gets sick and starts to die. You may have watched
a friend, a brother or sister, a grandparent or a parent die slowly and
over a period of time. You may have watched them lose their quality
of life.

You may also feel relief and release if you had a difficult relationship
with the person who died. We know a teen whose father died. His
father drank too much and wasn't easy to live with. When the father
died, the teen felt both a sense of relief and deep sadness. Other teens
who had been abused emotionally, physically or sexually by the person
who died typically feel relief and release after the death. This is
normal and natural.

My experience with feelings of relief is, or has been:

_____

_____

_____

_____

_____

_____

_____

_____

These are some of the common emotions you may feel as you journey through grief. You may also feel others that we haven't discussed. Are there any more feelings you've been having that you want to write about here? If so, go ahead.

_____

_____

_____

_____

_____

_____

_____

_____

As you move through your grief journey, over time and with the support of others, you will come to feel what we call "reconciliation." Reconciliation is the point at which you are able to fully enjoy life and living again. We'll talk more about this important goal on p. 83. In the meantime, we'd like to explain the six needs of mourning and how your grief journey will be affected by them.

58

UNDERSTANDING YOUR SIX NEEDS OF MOURNING

"There is only one happiness in life, to love and be loved."
George Sand

All of us, whether we are a child, a teen or an adult, have six central needs or "yield signs" to confront when someone in our life dies. This part of the journal will teach you about these needs and invite you to write out how they apply to your unique grief journey.

Oh, keep in mind that you will probably jump around in a random way while working on these six needs of mourning. Sometimes you will be working on more than one need at a time. Your awareness of these needs, however, will give you a great way to feel like you can do something to help yourself heal. While you have probably heard the saying, "Time heals all wounds," actually, only by working on these needs will your wounds heal!

The Six Needs of Mourning:

1. Accept the reality of the death.

2. Let yourself feel the pain of the loss.

3. Remember the person who died.

4. Develop a new self-identity.

5. Search for meaning.

6. Let others help you—now and always.

Need 1. Accept the reality of the death.

Someone you love has died and can never come back. That's a really hard thing to accept, but it's true. It may take you weeks, even months, to really accept the fact that this person is gone. It's normal for it to take that long.

First you'll come to accept the death intellectually, with your head. Only over time will you come to fully accept it with your heart. Now and then, especially at first, you may push away or feel the need to deny the reality to yourself. That's also normal. You'll accept the reality, bit by bit, as you're ready.

Express yourself!
Write out your thoughts and feelings about Need 1.

_____

_____

_____

_____

_____

_____

Where do you see yourself in accepting the reality of this death?

_____

_____

_____

_____

_____

_____

Do you think time is playing a part in where you are with this need? Yes_____ No_____ If so, how?

_____

_____

_____

_____

Do you understand and allow yourself the need to at times push some of the reality away? Yes_____ No_____
If so, how?

_____

_____

_____

_____

Is there someone you feel safe enough to talk with about this need and where you see yourself with it?
Yes_____ No_____ If so, who?_____

What do you think you would say to this person?

_____

_____

_____

_____

What can you do to continue to work on this need?

_____

_____

Need 2. Let yourself feel the pain of the loss.

You need to let yourself feel the pain of your loss. You need to feel it before you can heal it. Of course, it's easier to avoid, repress, deny or push away the pain of grief than it is to confront it. The problem is, confronting it is what tames it. If you don't confront it, it will lurk forever in your heart and soul.

You will probably need to "dose" yourself with your painful thoughts and feelings. In other words, you'll need to let just a little in at a time. If you were to try to allow in all the pain at once, you couldn't survive.

Express yourself!
Write out your thoughts and feelings about Need 2.

_____

_____

_____

_____

_____

_____

_____

_____

Where do you see yourself in feeling the pain of the loss?

_____

_____

_____

_____

_____

_____

_____

Do you think that time is playing a part in where you are with this need? Yes_____ No_____ If so, how?

_____

_____

_____

_____

Whom have you shared your feelings of hurt with?

_____

_____

_____

_____

Write about what sharing your feelings has been like for you.

_____

_____

_____

_____

_____

_____

_____

What can you do to continue to work on this need?

_____

_____

_____

_____

Need 3. Remember the person who died.

When someone you love dies, that person lives on in you through memory. To reconcile your loss, you need to actively remember the person who died and commemorate the life that was lived. We hope you have someone in your life who you feel safe to talk with about the person who died.

It's good to keep talking about the person who died. It's good to look at pictures of him or her. Never let anyone try to take away your memories in a misguided attempt to save you from pain. You need to remember, not forget. Remembering the past makes hoping for the future possible.

Some of the things that some teens do to keep memories alive are:

- talk with a special friend or family member about favorite memories you shared with the person who died.
- make a memory book or memory box (See Idea 75 in *Healing Your Grieving Heart for Teens.*)
- keep mementos of the person who died. A piece of jewelry, a favorite picture, an article of clothing or a special letter are just a few examples.
- visit places of special significance that help you remember times you spent together.
- look through photo albums at special times, such as birthdays, holidays, anniversaries or any other times you have a need to bring your memories closer to your heart.

We should also mention that memories are not always pleasant. If that applies to you, this need can be very hard. We encourage you to explore any painful memories with an adult you trust. You can also explore these kind of thoughts and feelings right here in your private journal.

Express yourself!
Write out your thoughts and feelings about Need 3.

_____

_____

_____

_____

_____

_____

_____

_____

_____

_____

_____

_____

_____

_____

_____

_____

_____

_____

_____

_____

_____

_____

_____

_____

_____

If you have another favorite picture of the person who died, put it right here in your journal:

Where do you see yourself in the process of remembering the person who died?

_____

_____

_____

_____

What is one of your favorite memories of the person who died?

_____

_____

_____

_____

_____

_____

_____

_____

What do you miss the very most about the person who died?

_____

_____

_____

_____

What do you miss the least about the person who died?

_____

_____

_____

_____

Can you recount a funny story about the person who died?

_____

_____

_____

_____

_____

_____

_____

_____

_____

_____

_____

_____

_____

_____

_____

Do you have people around you who are helping you remember this person? Yes_____ No_____ If so, please explain who they are and how they help you remember.

_____

_____

_____

_____

_____

_____

_____

_____

What are examples of things you have done to keep alive memories of the person who died?

_____

_____

_____

_____

_____

_____

_____

_____

_____

_____

_____

_____

What can you do to continue to work on this need?

_____

_____

_____

_____

_____

_____

_____

_____

_____

_____

Pick up a pen or pencil and write the name of the person who has died in the space below as many times as possible. As you fill the page, think of all your memories of this special person.

Need 4. Develop a new self-identity.

The person who died was part of who you are. Part of your identity came from this person. Let's say your best friend was Mary and she died. You probably thought of yourself not only as a student, a son or daughter, a brother or sister, but also as "Mary's best friend." Others thought of you in this way, too.

The way you defined yourself and the way society defined you has changed. Now you need to re-adjust your self-identity, to re-anchor yourself. This is really hard, especially if the person who died played a big part in your life.

Express yourself!
Write out your thoughts and feelings about Need 4.

_____

_____

_____

_____

_____

_____

_____

_____

Where do you see yourself in developing a new self-identity?

_____

_____

_____

_____

_____

What roles did the person who died play in your life?

_____

_____

_____

_____

What identity changes have you experienced as a result of this death?

_____

_____

_____

_____

How do you see people treating you differently as a result of your changed identity?

_____

_____

_____

_____

Do you ever feel like this new identity has you feeling like you want to be younger or older than you really are?
Yes_____ No_____ If so, how?

_____

_____

_____

_____

_____

Do you have a support system that understands your changed identity? Yes_____ No_____
If so, how do they let you know that they understand your changed identity?

_____
_____
_____
_____
_____
_____
_____

Which, if any, positive changes in your self-identity have you noticed since the death?

_____
_____
_____
_____
_____
_____
_____

What can you do to continue to work on this need?

_____
_____
_____
_____
_____

Need 5. Search for meaning.

When someone we love dies, we naturally question the meaning and purpose of life and death. Why do people die? Why did this person have to die? What happens to people after they die? Why am I still alive? What's life for? This may be the first time in your life that you've really thought about these questions. And questions just don't get any harder than these.

Nobody really knows all the answers to these kinds of questions, not even grown-ups. But it's OK to ask adults you care about and trust what they think. Some adults have lived enough, loved enough, experienced enough and pondered enough to have some pretty good ideas. Also, some of your best friends might be good listeners to your "search for meaning" questions. Hearing what they think and feel might help you not feel so alone with these questions. Writing out what you think and feel in your very own journal can also help.

Express yourself!
Write out your thoughts and feelings about Need 5.

_____

_____

_____

_____

_____

Where do you see yourself in your search for meaning?

_____

_____

_____

_____

_____

What were your spiritual or religious beliefs about life and death before this death?

_____

_____

_____

_____

_____

_____

_____

Have these beliefs been changed by this death?

Yes_____ No_____ Please explain.

_____

_____

_____

_____

_____

_____

Do you have any "Why?" or "How?" questions right now?

Yes_____ No_____ If so, what are they?

_____

_____

_____

_____

_____

_____

_____

Do you feel like it is OK that you have these "search for meaning" questions? Yes_____ No_____
Please explain.

_____
_____
_____
_____

Do you ever feel like you are "treading water" or "standing still" in your search for meaning? Yes_____ No_____
Please explain.

_____
_____
_____
_____

Identify below which trusted friends or caring adults you could talk about your "meaning of life and death" questions with. Please explain why you feel safe to talk with these people.

_____
_____
_____
_____

What can you do to continue to work on this need?

_____
_____

Express yourself through prayer

Studies have shown that prayer can help people heal. If you believe in a higher power, the space below is a safe place for you to write out a prayer.

You can pray about the person who died. You can pray about your questions about life and death. You can pray for help in dealing with the pain you feel. You can pray for others affected by this death.

Dear God,

_____

_____

_____

_____

_____

_____

_____

_____

_____

_____

_____

_____

_____

_____

_____

_____

Need 6. Let others help you—now and always.

When you're a teenager, it's natural to want adults to keep out of your face. You're getting old enough now that you don't need or want their help with every little thing, right? We agree with you. Growing up means finding your own way and doing things on your own.

But, grief isn't an "on your own" kind of experience. It's probably the hardest work anyone ever has to do. And you just can't do it all on your own. While journaling can be a big help, we also want to encourage you to talk to adults who care about you. If you don't want to talk to them, at least let them talk to you. Or hang out with them without talking. Talk to your friends, instead. Or, if it feels right for you, join a support group with other teens who have also experienced the death of someone in their lives. Write notes or e-mail your thoughts and feelings to someone you don't have to look at every day.

Express yourself!
Write out your thoughts and feelings about Need 6.

_____

_____

_____

_____

_____

_____

Where do you see yourself on letting others help you, now and always?

_____

_____

_____

_____

Whom do you turn to for help?

_____

_____

_____

_____

What do these people do that lets you know they are there to support you?

_____

_____

_____

_____

How are you doing with accepting support from people who try to give it?

_____

_____

_____

_____

Is there anybody trying to give you help that you wish would just leave you alone? Yes_____ No_____

Who?_____

Why do you want them to leave you alone?

_____

_____

_____

_____

Some teens have a real hard time accepting support from adults. How about you? What is your experience with this?

_____

_____

_____

_____

_____

_____

Are you getting support from other teens who have had deaths? Yes_____ No_____ Please explain.

_____

_____

_____

_____

_____

_____

When you have a "griefburst"—which is a sudden and unexpected wave of sadness over the death—are people supportive? Yes_____ No_____ Please explain.

_____

_____

_____

_____

_____

_____

Are you compassionate with yourself when you have these "griefbursts"? Yes_____ No_____ Please explain.

_____

_____

_____

_____

_____

_____

_____

What can you do to continue to work on this need?

_____

_____

_____

_____

_____

_____

_____

Final Thoughts About These Important Six Needs

We have outlined these Six Needs of Mourning to remind you that you can work on them to help yourself heal. Your needs will continue to change as you allow yourself to openly and honestly mourn. From time to time, you may want to return to this section of your journal and revisit the six needs. A lot of teens have taught us that they actually enjoy going back to these needs and seeing their progress. Drop us an e-mail (wolfelt@centerforloss.com) and let us know where you see yourself now and in the future. We will write back!

HOW YOU'LL KNOW YOU'RE HEALING: RECONCILIATION

"Hope is grief's best music."
Proverb

As you know by now, grief and mourning are powerful experiences. So is your ability to help yourself heal (to "become whole"). In doing the work of mourning by filling in this journal, you are moving toward your healing.

But, it's important to remember that everyone grieves in different ways and different times. There is no set timetable for grief. You may feel that you're healing six months, a year or two years after losing someone special. Then one day you might feel incredibly sad or lonely because you miss that person so very much. Know that this is normal. Both of us have experienced this very thing!

In our experience, everyone is changed by the experience of grief—children, teens like you, and yes, even adults. You are changed. The death of someone loved alters your life forever. The issue is not that you will never be happy again. It is simply that you will never be exactly the same as you were before the death. I, Alan, thought I was going to grow up to be an architect or attorney and I grew up to be a grief counselor and author. Megan thinks she is going to grow up to be in the creative arts—probably an actress. But who knows? We'll wait and see where the journey of life takes her. How about you? What do you think you want to do when you "grow up?"

Please remember that healing in grief is often a two-steps-forward/one-step-back process. You will never completely "get over" the death, but you will, over time and with the support of others, learn to reconcile yourself to it.

Healing is not a perfect state of "recovery" or "resolution." You can and probably will have pangs of grief years after the death. That revisiting of painful feelings doesn't mean anything is wrong with you. Healing does not mean forgetting.

In exploring what your eventual healing goal will and can be, we ask you to consider using the term "reconciliation." We believe this term is more expressive of what occurs as you work to integrate the new reality of moving forward in your life without the physical presence of the person who has died.

If you do the hard work of mourning, as you are doing by using this journal, you can and will experience reconciliation, which consists of:

• a renewed sense of energy and confidence.
• an ability to acknowledge the full reality of the death.
• the capacity to enjoy experiences in life that are normally enjoyable.
• the ability to organize and plan your life toward the future, while still remembering your past.
• the awareness that you have allowed yourself to fully grieve and mourn, and you have survived.
• the ability to love and be loved.
• the capacity to get to know new parts of yourself that you have discovered in your grief journey.

Yes, if you keep embracing your grief and sharing it outside yourself, you can and will come to this reconciliation. As you do this work, your painful thoughts and feelings will soften and grow less frequent. Instead of being ever-present, sharp and stinging, they will be occasional and more dull and mellow.

In the space below, take this opportunity to write out where you see yourself in your own unique healing process right now. As you have read and learned about the concept of reconciliation, what thoughts and feelings come to you?

_____

_____

_____

_____

_____

_____

_____

_____

_____

_____

_____

_____

_____

_____

_____

_____

_____

_____

_____

_____

_____

_____

Place a favorite picture of yourself smiling below. Yes, your grief has made you sad, but we want you to remember that you can and will be happy again.

MEMORIES: CAPTURING, TREASURING, LIVING ON

"Life must be lived forward, but remembered backward."
Soren Kierkegaard

What remains of a person's life here on earth after he or she has died? A few physical items survive—clothing, keepsakes, photos. These are wonderful treasures to comfort us when we need comfort. But the most important thing a person leaves behind is inside you—your memories of his or her life. We've included this section in the journal because we want you to capture as many memories as you can for posterity. Years later, when your memory's no longer so sharp, you'll be so glad you wrote them down. We also want you to experience memory's healing touch. At first your memories may feel painful to you. But over time, the more you remember, the more you'll be able to integrate the loss into your continued life. And the happier you'll be.

In this section we've also included space for you to consider how you can turn your memories into memorials—in other words, how you can help perpetuate the legacy of the person who died. You can do many things to pay ongoing tribute. You can do many things to continue to demonstrate your love. Be creative and be committed.

Place another favorite photo of the person who died (or, if you'd prefer, mementos such as ticket stubs, programs, newspaper clippings, etc.) in the space below.

Even though we asked you this before, write out again:
What do you miss most about the person who died? I miss....

_____

_____

_____

_____

_____

_____

_____

_____

_____

_____

What do you miss the least about the person who died?
I don't miss. . .

_____

_____

_____

_____

_____

_____

_____

_____

_____

_____

Write out below a funny or meaningful story about the person who died.

_____

_____

_____

_____

_____

_____

_____

_____

_____

_____

_____

_____

_____

_____

_____

_____

_____

_____

_____

_____

_____

_____

_____

_____

What other things will you always remember about the person who died?

_____

_____

_____

_____

_____

_____

What would you want others to always remember about the person who died?

_____

_____

_____

_____

_____

_____

When you look up in the sky and you think about the person who died, what thoughts and feelings come up for you?

_____

_____

_____

_____

_____

_____

What I learned most from the person who died about love was . . .

_____

_____

_____

_____

_____

_____

_____

A time the person who died encouraged me was . . .

_____

_____

_____

_____

_____

_____

_____

Other ways the person who died was supportive to me were . . .

_____

_____

_____

_____

_____

_____

Sayings the person who died used to say are . . .

_____

_____

_____

_____

The most important thing I learned from the person who
died was . . .

_____

_____

_____

_____

_____

_____

The best advice I ever got from the person who died was . . .

_____

_____

_____

_____

_____

Some things I'd really like to say to the person who
died are . . .

_____

_____

_____

_____

In the space below, write a letter to the person who died. Tell him or her what is in your head and on your heart.

Dear _____,

_____
_____
_____
_____
_____
_____
_____
_____
_____
_____
_____
_____
_____
_____
_____
_____
_____
_____
_____
_____
_____
_____
_____
_____
_____
_____
_____

In the space below, imagine the person who died could write a letter back to you. What do you think he or she would want to say to you?

Dear _____,

_____

_____

_____

_____

_____

_____

_____

_____

_____

_____

_____

_____

_____

_____

_____

_____

_____

_____

_____

_____

_____

_____

_____

_____

_____

_____

_____

_____

A Sunrise Remembrance

Getting up early to watch the sun splash color across the sky can change your whole outlook and help you feel close to the person who died. The sun is a powerful symbol of life and renewal. Getting up extra early once in a while also allows you to have a special time of quiet and solitude to honor the life of the person who died.

After you have watched the sunrise and reflected on the life of the person who died as well as your relationship to him or her, write out your thoughts and feelings below:

_____

_____

_____

_____

_____

_____

_____

_____

_____

_____

_____

_____

_____

_____

_____

_____

Memorialize the Person Who Died

You can probably remember the person who died in lots of different ways. Reflecting on her special qualities may make you sad at first, but this is a good way to keep her spirit alive and honor her life. Was he or she understanding? Funny? Artistic? Smart?

Choose your favorite characteristics then think of a tangible way to express them. Pour yourself into creating something that will be a tribute to the person who died. You could paint a painting, write a poem, build a garden bench, volunteer in his or her honor, walk in a memory walk—anything that pays tribute to his or her unique life is fitting. Then, write about what you did. Tape in a photo if you'd like, too.

_____

_____

_____

_____

_____

_____

_____

_____

_____

_____

_____

_____

_____

Listen to the Music of Memories

Music touches the heart of many teens. Try to collect at least three pieces of music that speak to you, or help you remember the person who died. After you have noted the selection, write out why you think this music speaks to your soul about your special person.

Song #1_____
Why it's meaningful to me

_____

_____

_____

_____

Song #2_____
Why it's meaningful to me

_____

_____

_____

_____

Song #3_____
Why it's meaningful to me

_____

_____

_____

_____

GETTING TO KNOW YOURSELF: THE REAL YOU

"The foundation of a person is not in matter but in spirit."
Ralph Waldo Emerson

When someone in our life dies, we sometimes say, "I lost someone." In reality, what we are really feeling is, "I am lost." When someone we love dies, we lose our sense of who we are in the world. We lose our identity in relationship to the "mirror" in our life. An important part of mourning is to search for who we are and who we will become in the face of this loss.

This section of the journal is intended to encourage you to look at who you are and how you see yourself. First we start with a few questions in which you look at yourself in comparison to the person who died. Then we move on to questions just about you—what you're like, what you care about, what gives your life meaning. Enjoy!

Place a photo of yourself here. Years later, when you look back at this journal, it'll be fun for you to remember what you looked like at this time.

You and the person who died probably had some things in common and some things not in common. The following activity will help you explore favorite things for both of you. If you don't know the answer to some of these, ask people who can help you.

Favorites

	(name of person who died)	(your name)
Hobby	_____	_____
Food	_____	_____
Color	_____	_____
Movie	_____	_____
Book	_____	_____
Season	_____	_____
Vacation	_____	_____
Game	_____	_____
Place	_____	_____
Music	_____	_____
Sport	_____	_____
Clothes	_____	_____

What did you have in common? How were you different?
As you can see, you can still love somebody even if they're
different than you.

How was the person who died like you?

_____

_____

_____

How was the person who died different than you?

_____

_____

_____

How would you describe yourself to a friend?

_____

_____

_____

What makes you happy?

_____

_____

_____

What makes you mad?

_____

_____

_____

What makes you sad?

_____

_____

_____

The best thing I know about me is . . .

_____

_____

_____

I feel good about myself when . . .

_____

_____

_____

I dream that one day I will . . .

_____

_____

_____

When I'm feeling down, a few things I can do to help
myself feel better are . . .

_____

_____

_____

_____

_____

The hardest thing about growing up for me has been . . .

_____

_____

_____

When I think about my time at school, I think about . . .

_____

_____

_____

Describe your family :

_____

_____

_____

What is it like to live in your family?

_____

_____

_____

Name six things that you love

_____   _____

_____   _____

_____   _____

Write down one of your favorite song lyrics:

_____

_____

What is it about you that makes people like you? Why do
your friends enjoy being with you?

_____

_____

_____

_____

Do you consider yourself to be a leader or a follower?
Explain.

_____

_____

_____

_____

Write about something you like doing. How did you get
interested in this? Why do you think you like it so much?

_____

_____

_____

_____

_____

Describe how you are different now than you were two
years ago.

_____

_____

_____

_____

Make a list of three important changes in your life, such as going from grade school to middle school, losing a best friend or moving to a new house or city. What have you learned from these experiences?

1._____

_____

2._____

_____

3._____

_____

Make a list of things you are thankful for:

_____   _____

_____   _____

_____   _____

_____   _____

_____   _____

_____   _____

_____   _____

_____   _____

_____   _____

_____   _____

_____   _____

_____   _____

_____   _____

Write about what's in your heart and soul:

_____

_____

_____

_____

_____

_____

_____

_____

_____

_____

_____

_____

_____

_____

_____

_____

_____

_____

_____

_____

_____

_____

_____

Writing about these things can help you see where you are and where you're going. Won't it be fun to look back years from now and read what you have written!

TAKING CARE OF YOURSELF:
THE TEEN MOURNER'S CODE

"It is good to have an end to journey toward, but it is the journey that matters in the end."
Ursula K. Le Guin

Though you should reach out to others as you journey through grief, you shouldn't feel obligated to accept the unhelpful responses you may receive from some people. You have certain "rights" no one should try to take away from you.

The following principles are intended to both empower you to heal and to help you decide how others can and cannot help. You will notice that many of the guidelines have already been referred to in the journal. The repetition and summary of these principles is intentional. Even after you have completed this journal, we encourage you to reread this Mourner's Code occasionally.

You will see that following each principle we have left a place for you to "Express Yourself" with any thoughts and feelings that come to your head and heart.

1. I have the right to have my own unique feelings about the death. I may feel mad, sad or lonely. I may feel scared or relieved. I may feel numb or sometimes not anything at all. No one will feel exactly like I do.

Express yourself:

_____

_____

_____

_____

2. I have the right to talk about my grief whenever I feel like talking. When I need to talk, I will find someone who will listen to me and love me. When I don't want to talk about it, that's OK, too.

Express yourself:

_____

_____

_____

_____

3. I have the right to show my feelings of grief in my own way. When they are hurting, some teens like to have fun so they'll feel better for awhile. I can play games, hang out with my friends and laugh, too. I might also get mad and scream. This does not mean I am bad, it just means I have scary feelings that I need help with.

Express yourself:

_____

_____

_____

_____

4. I have the right to need other people to help me with my grief, especially grown-ups who care about me. Mostly I need them to pay attention to what I am feeling and saying and to love me no matter what.

Express yourself:

_____

_____

_____

_____

5. I have the right to get upset about normal, everyday problems.
I might feel grumpy and have trouble getting along with
others sometimes.

Express yourself:

_____

_____

_____

_____

6. I have the right to have "griefbursts." Griefbursts are sudden,
unexpected feelings of sadness that just hit me sometimes—even
long after the death. These feelings can be very strong and even
scary. When this happens, I might not want to be alone.

Express yourself:

_____

_____

_____

_____

7. I have the right to use my beliefs about God to help me deal with
my feelings of grief. Praying might make me feel better and
somehow closer to the person who died.

Express yourself:

_____

_____

_____

_____

8. I have the right to try to figure out why the person I loved died. But it's OK if I don't find an answer. "Why" questions about life and death are the hardest questions in the world.

Express yourself:

_____

_____

_____

_____

9. I have the right to think and talk about my memories of the person who died. Sometimes those memories will be happy and sometimes they might be sad. Either way, these memories help me keep alive my love for the person who died.

Express yourself:

_____

_____

_____

_____

10. I have the right to move toward and feel my grief and, over time, to heal. I'll go on to live a happy life, but the life and death of the person who died will always be a part of me. I'll always miss the person who died.

Express yourself:

_____

_____

_____

_____

A FINAL WORD

We believe that every human being, including teens like you, wants to "mourn well" the death of someone loved. It is as essential as breathing. Some people make the choice to give momentum to their mourning, while others deny or avoid it.

By choosing to work through this journal, you have moved toward your grief and mourning. As you continue to actively mourn this death, you can look forward to the days to come when your grief won't be so hard. Your painful feelings of loss will soften and slowly be overtaken by warm thoughts and memories of times you spent with the person who died.

Yes, grief is indeed a wise teacher. Grief teaches us that there is so much to know about ourselves and the world around us. Grief teaches us that we need to pay attention, to simplify our lives to be open to giving and receiving love.

Grief teaches us that loving and caring for others are our most important tasks here on earth. Grief teaches us we have only now to let people know that we love them. There is magic and miracles in loving and being loved.

We hope we meet you one day and that you will tell us what grief has taught you. Until then, mourn well.

And just one more thing: Right now, take a moment to close your eyes, open your heart and remember that special smile of the person who died.

YOUR CONTINUING JOURNEY: REFLECTIONS AS YOU GROW

We invite you to use the rest of these pages to revisit your journey through grief in the months and years to come. Every six months or so, come back to this journal and write down your current thoughts and feelings about the death. Be well and mourn well.

ALSO BY ALAN WOLFELT

HEALING YOUR GRIEVING HEART FOR TEENS: 100 PRACTICAL IDEAS

Grief is especially difficult during the teen years. This book explains why this is so and offers straightforward, practical advice for healing.

ISBN 1-879651-23-8
128 pages • Softcover • $11.95

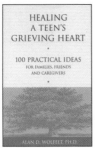

HEALING A TEEN'S GRIEVING HEART: 100 PRACTICAL IDEAS FOR FAMILIES, FRIENDS & CAREGIVERS

If you want to help a grieving teen but aren't sure how, this book is for you. It explains the teen's unique mourning needs, offers real-world advice and suggests realistic activities.

ISBN 1-879651-24-6
128 pages • Softcover • $11.95
(plus additional shipping and handling)

Companion
PRESS

All Dr. Wolfelt's publications can be ordered by mail from:
Companion Press
3735 Broken Bow Road • Fort Collins, CO 80526
(970) 226-6050 • Fax 1-800-922-6051
www.centerforloss.com